The Girl in the White Dress
A Place Between Two Worlds

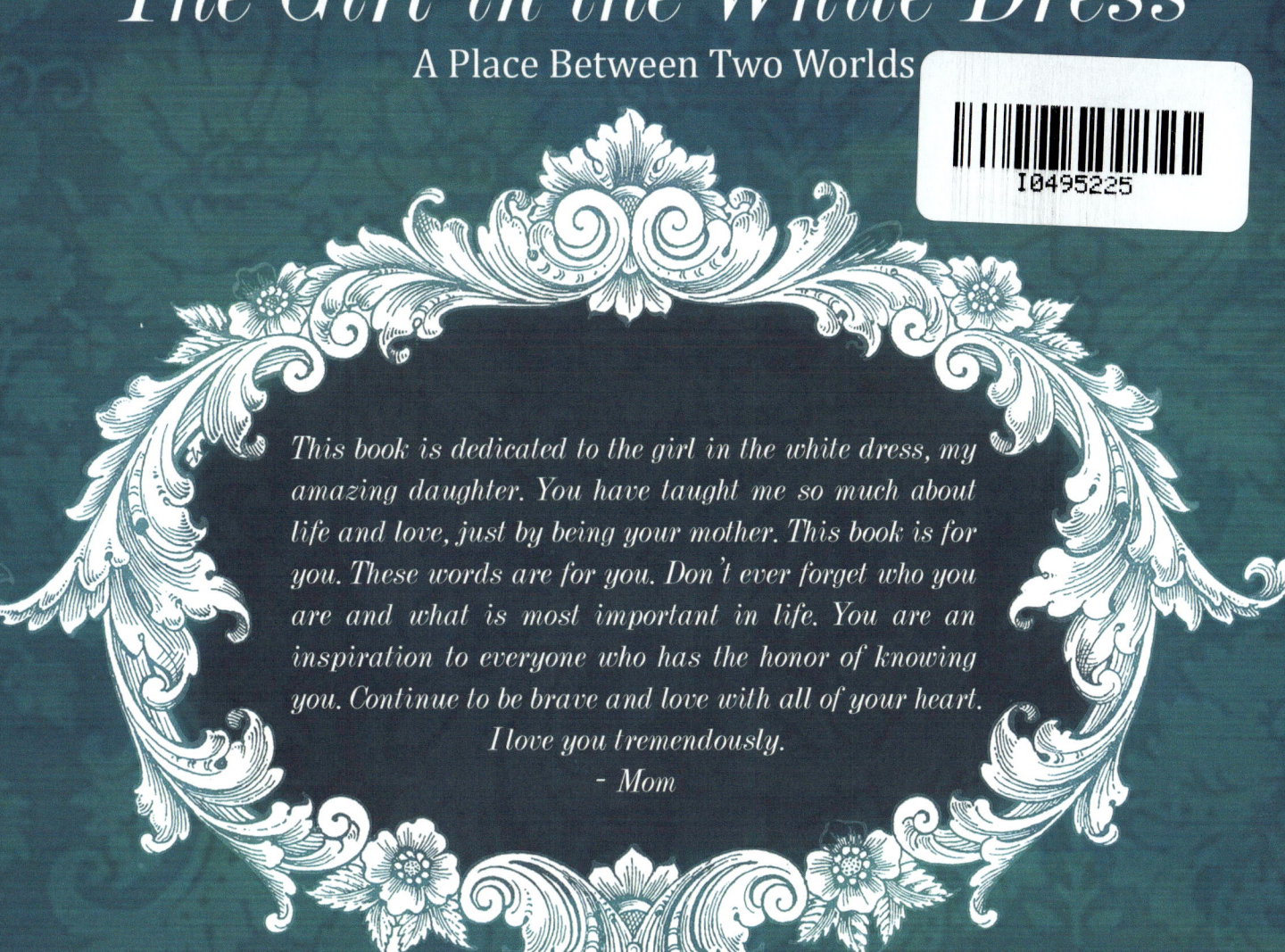

This book is dedicated to the girl in the white dress, my amazing daughter. You have taught me so much about life and love, just by being your mother. This book is for you. These words are for you. Don't ever forget who you are and what is most important in life. You are an inspiration to everyone who has the honor of knowing you. Continue to be brave and love with all of your heart. I love you tremendously.
- Mom

by Jessica Hatlen

"Edge of the World"

My Dear Girl,

We spend so much of our life in a balancing act. Balancing careers and family, schedules, emotions. The list is endless. So many of us stay teetering on the edge for so long, that we are almost suspended in limbo. Just balancing because that is all we know how to do or we are too afraid to jump off. What happens when we decide to take the leap? What happens when we stop our balancing and jump in feet first into something different, something maybe outside of our comfort zone? Growth happens. self discovery happens. inspiration develops. Sometimes we have to take that chance, or live the rest of our lives wondering what if. It's ok to be scared of what leaping brings, but always remember to have faith in the process and don't ever be afraid to chase your dreams. Great things can not happen if you spend all your time focusing on the balancing act.

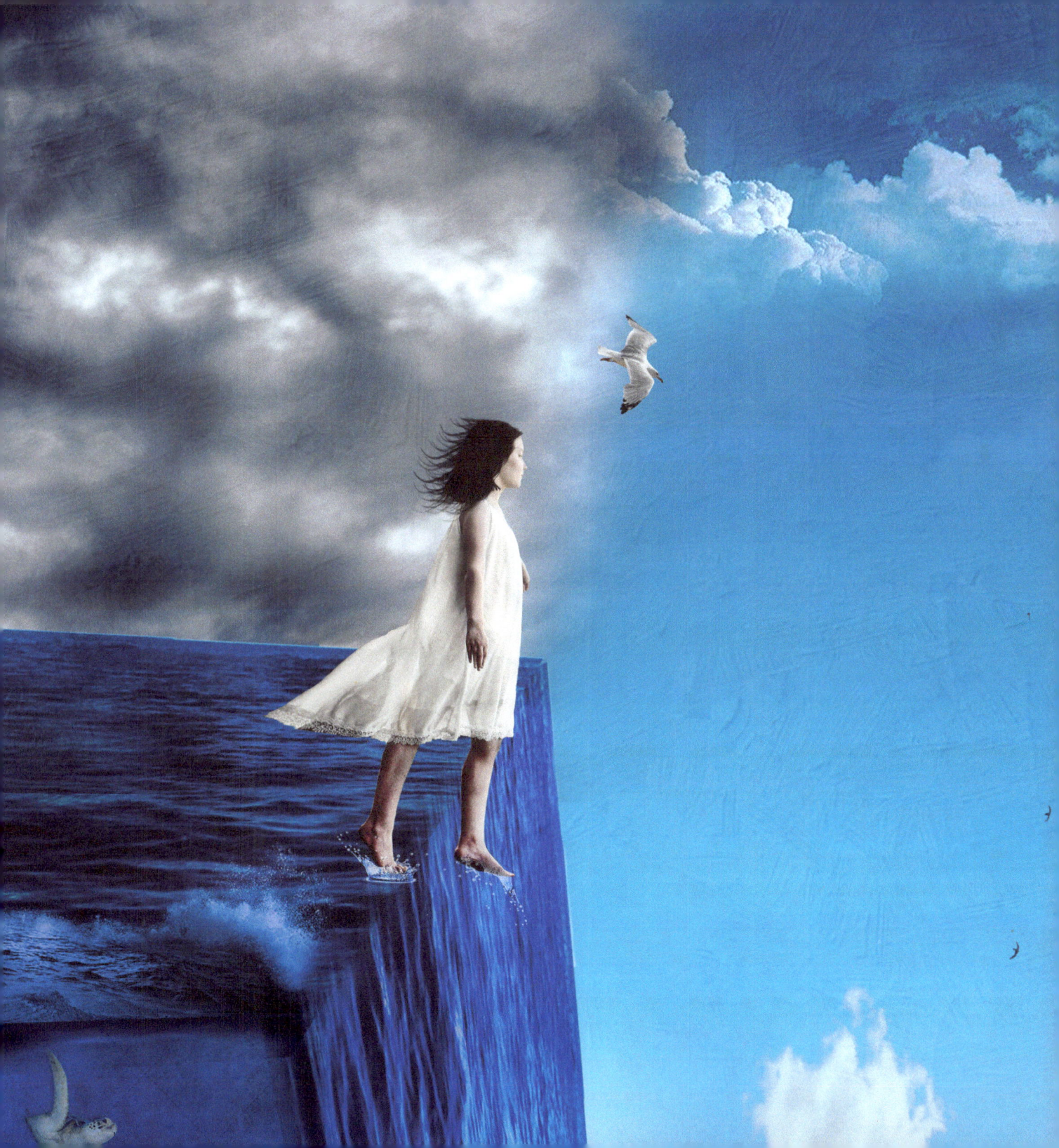

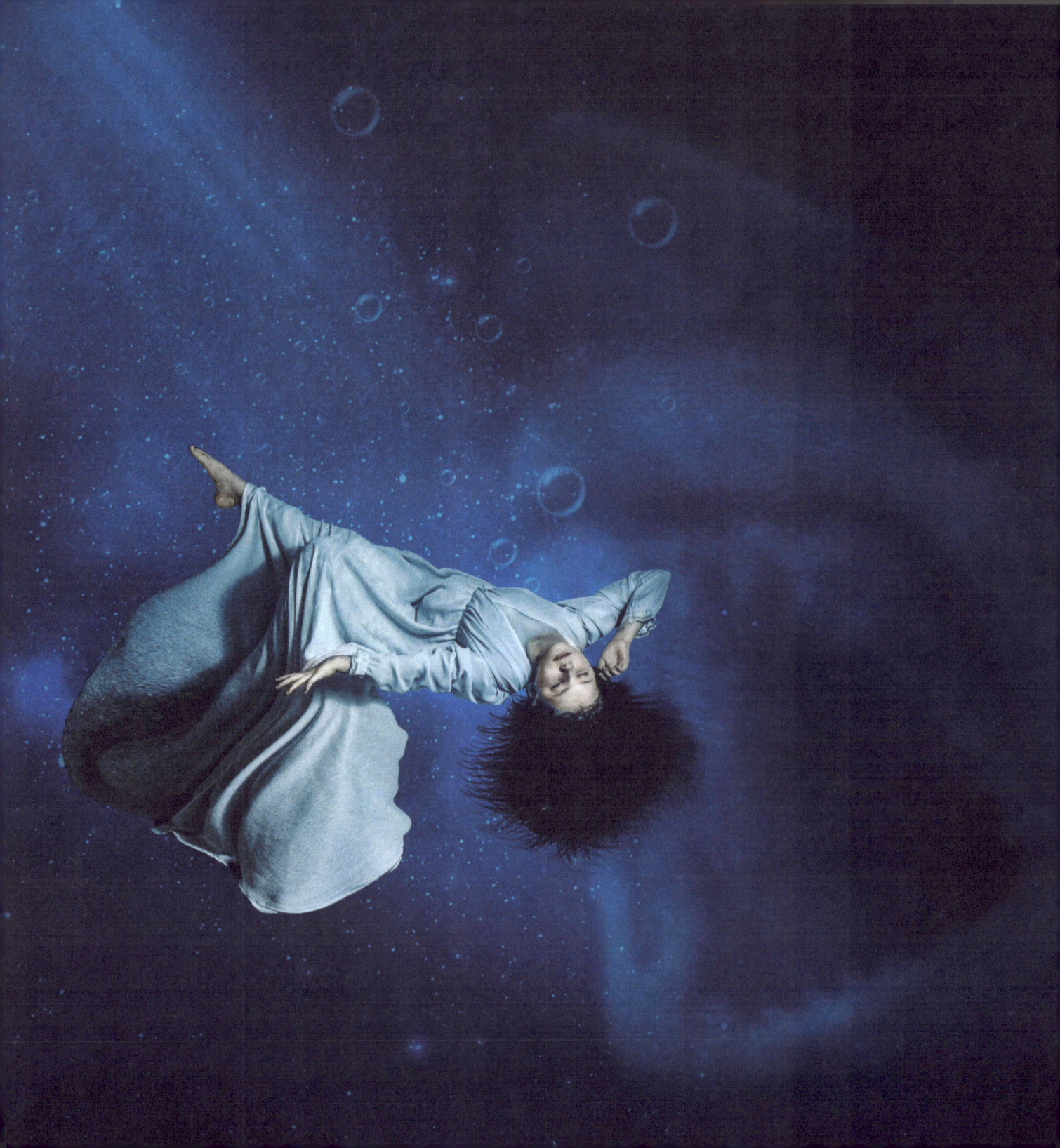

"Angst"

My Brave Girl,

Anxiety is something we all experience. It lurks in the corner of self doubt and worry, like a monster in the dark, and if we are not careful it can swallow us whole. Just know that in these moments, where you feel you are just floating in between worlds, with the fear of what lurks in the darkness, YOU are filled with an extraordinary light and strength that will shine through in even the darkest of days. Don't allow yourself to forget who you are. Remember that how you are feeling, is just how you feel right now, and that it won't last forever. Don't let the anxiety and fear swallow you up. You are stronger than those thoughts and worries. You are full of light and are loved beyond measure.

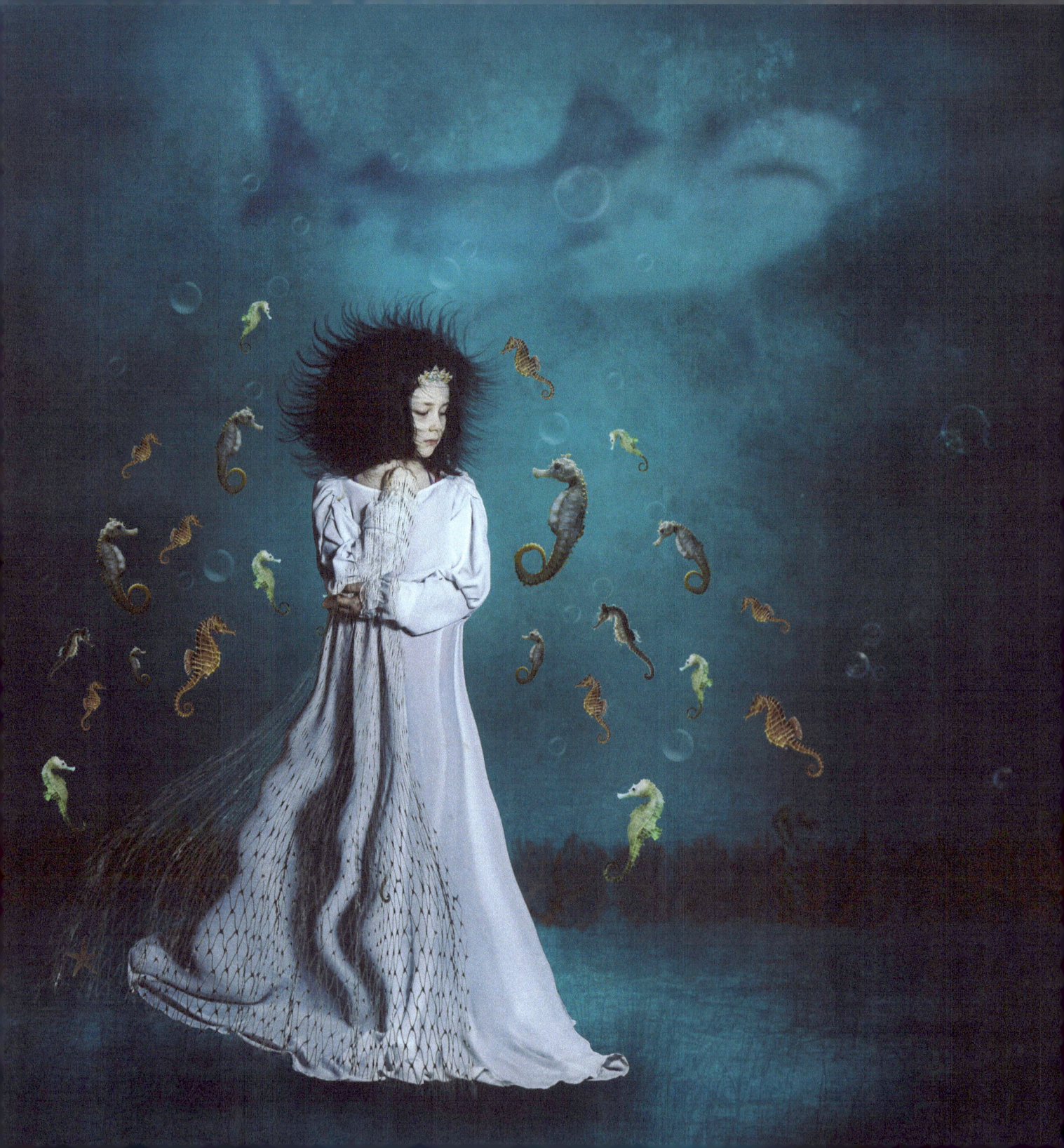

"Friendship"

My Caring Girl,

Many people will come in and out of your life. Those that you think are important to you now, may not always be there tomorrow. Find your tribe. Your select few people who see you for you. Who love you for your strengths, your weaknesses, your caring nature, and can support you through life's ups and downs. The number of people you surround yourself with will never be as important as the quality of people you surround yourself with. Don't forget that. Not everyone who appears in your circle will be worthy of being there. You will find through life that many times there are sharks lurking in the waters, waiting for their chance to drag you down. Let those people go, and remember that those who know and love you the most are the people you invest your time into. The only people in this life who matter, are the ones that you allow to matter. Never lose that caring nature, but always be aware that there are people who will try to take advantage of it. Don't let those people take from you the beauty that is love.

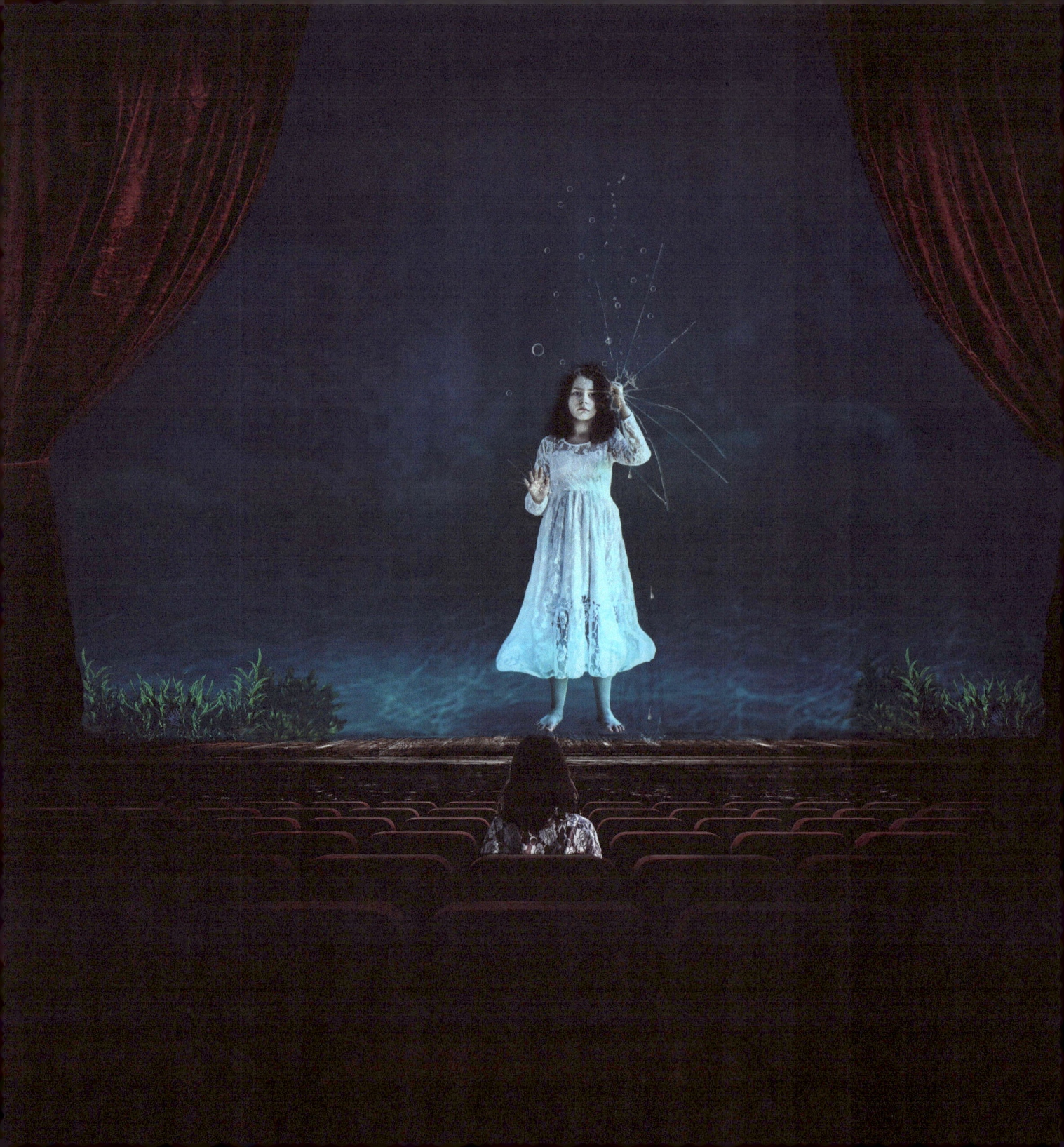

"The Show"

My Observant Girl,

As we grow older, we have to learn to adapt to our surroundings. The world will try to mold us into a more uniform shape, to do the song and dances that others want to see us do. That is not your mold. Yes, the world's a stage, and every choice you make will be seen by others, no matter how small or seemingly unimportant. Don't allow yourself to be trapped by other's expectations. Always be true to yourself, otherwise you will find that you are just a spectator in your own life. The only show you will ever have to put on will be of your choosing. You are the writer of your story, no one else is. Don't ever forget that. Live each day to make yourself proud of who you are. Whether there is a full auditorium watching, or you are sitting alone. Your voice and story is important.

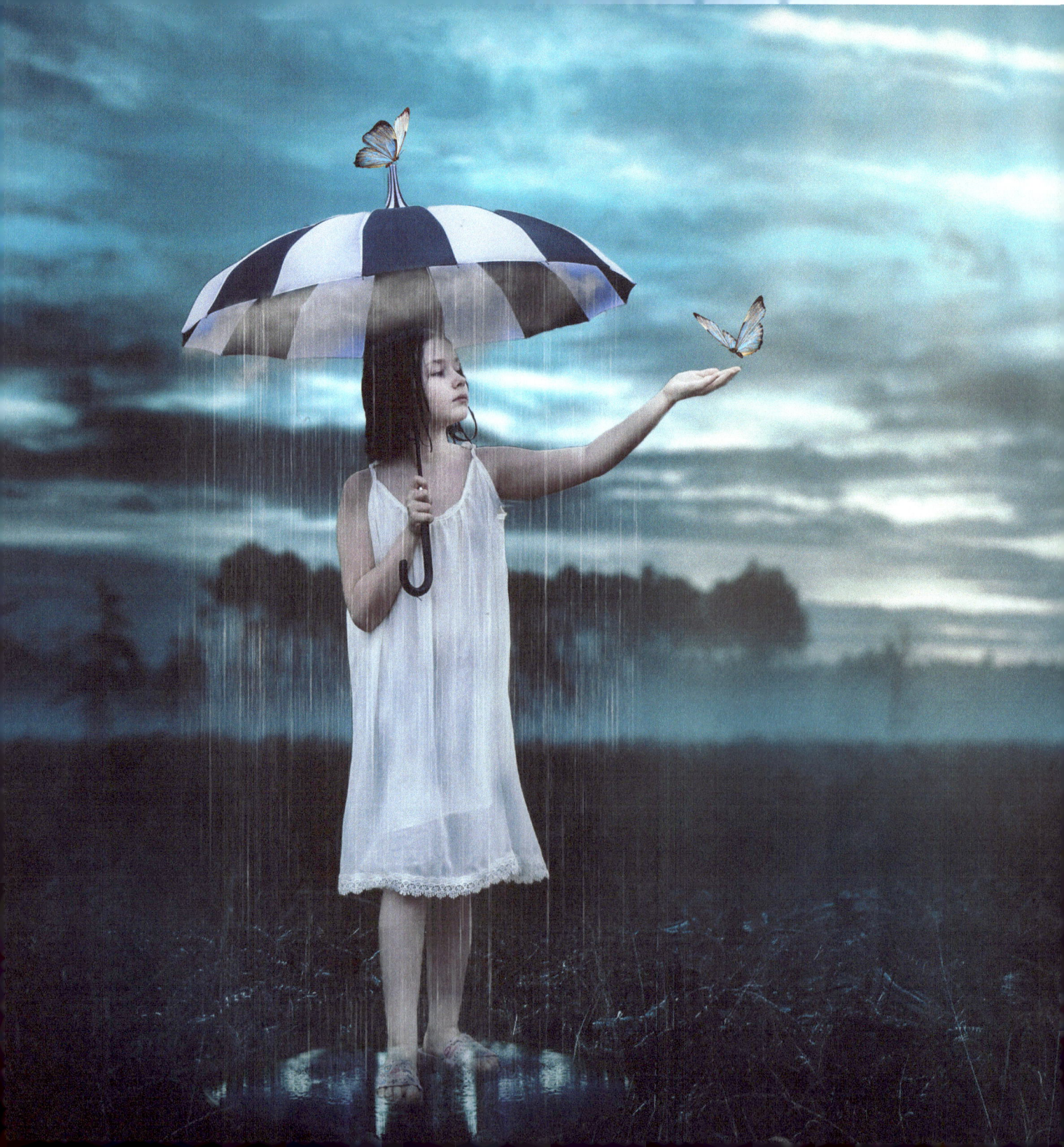

"Rainy Days"

My Emotional Girl,

Some days it is hard to see the sun through all the rain. Those days are part of life, and part of growth. Just know that if it is raining on you now, the sun will eventually shine it's way through and these days will be a fleeting memory. Always look for that light, even on the rainiest of days. It is there if you look. It is ok to be caught in the storm of your own worry and doubt, that is part of the human experience. Just don't allow yourself to stay there. See it for what it is, shake off the drops of rain, and step yourself out of the storm. Don't allow yourself to seek comfort in that rain, for when you are comfortable and caught up in so many rainy days, it is hard to seek the warmth and light. It's ok to feel emotions, and it is ok to feel sad, but don't let it consume you and that beautiful light you shine.

"The Dreamer"

My Visionary Girl,

We will not always be where we want to be in life. It is part of growing up and learning who we are. Promise me, that when you realize there is a place you would rather be, that you stay true to yourself, and you push to make it to that place. The only thing that holds us back in this world is ourselves. If you are unhappy with your life, unhappy with where you are, instead of dreaming of the change, make it happen. You are capable of extraordinary things in this life. Your dreaming spirit shows you daily how full of possibilities this life truly is. You deserve all of these amazing things, and you can make it happen. You are a dreamer, a visionary, and you are driven. Nothing will hold you back from being who you are meant to be. If you can envision it, than it can be yours. Have faith in yourself, and know that I have complete faith in you.

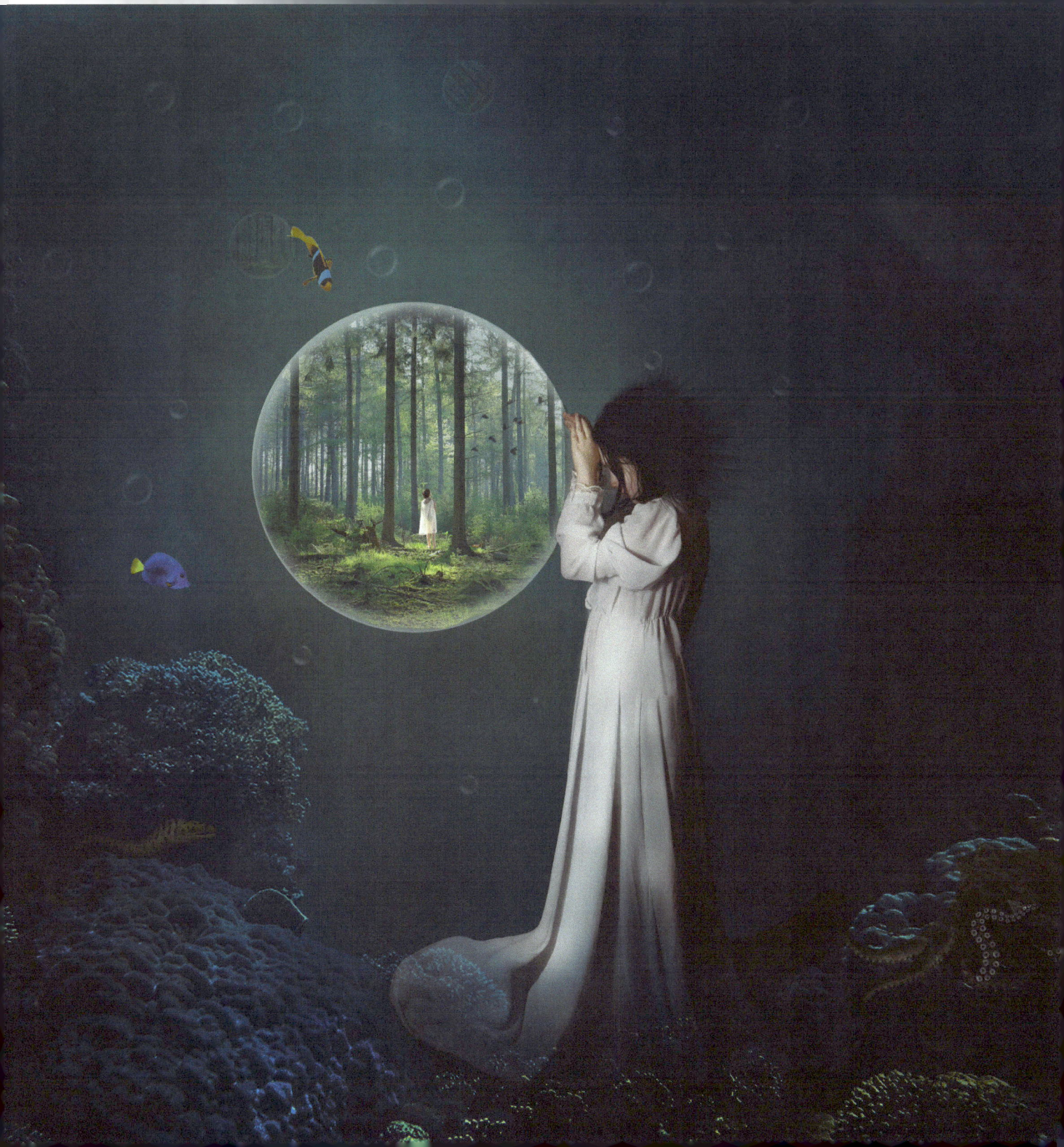

"The Window"

My Solitary Girl

The world can be a lonely place. Especially if you allow yourself to just be a spectator. Standing in your window, watching the world pass you by. Don't allow yourself to waste away. You are capable of doing great things in this world, but you have to participate to accomplish those goals. I know that it is safe in your window, but sometimes life involves taking chances, of getting outside of our comfort zone and pushing ourselves to do things we never thought possible. I promise you that as long as you keep pushing yourself outside of your comfort zone, you will see the most beautiful things life has to offer. Yes, there will be times that will not be easy, but those are the times we need to experience so that we know and appreciate when the good times are happening. Don't be afraid to live your life. Do not lock yourself away out of fear or uncertainty. You were designed to be capable of changing the world.

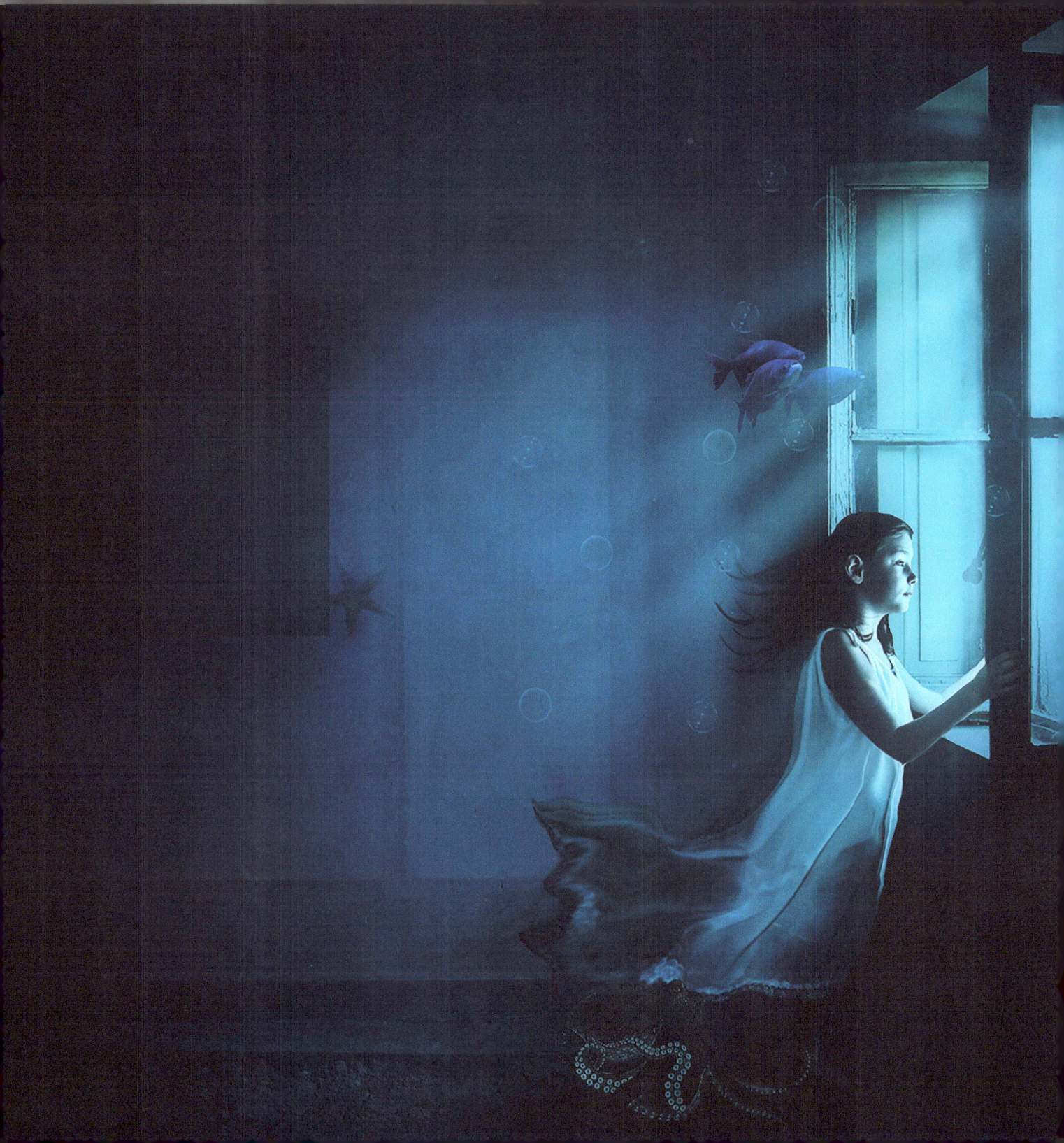

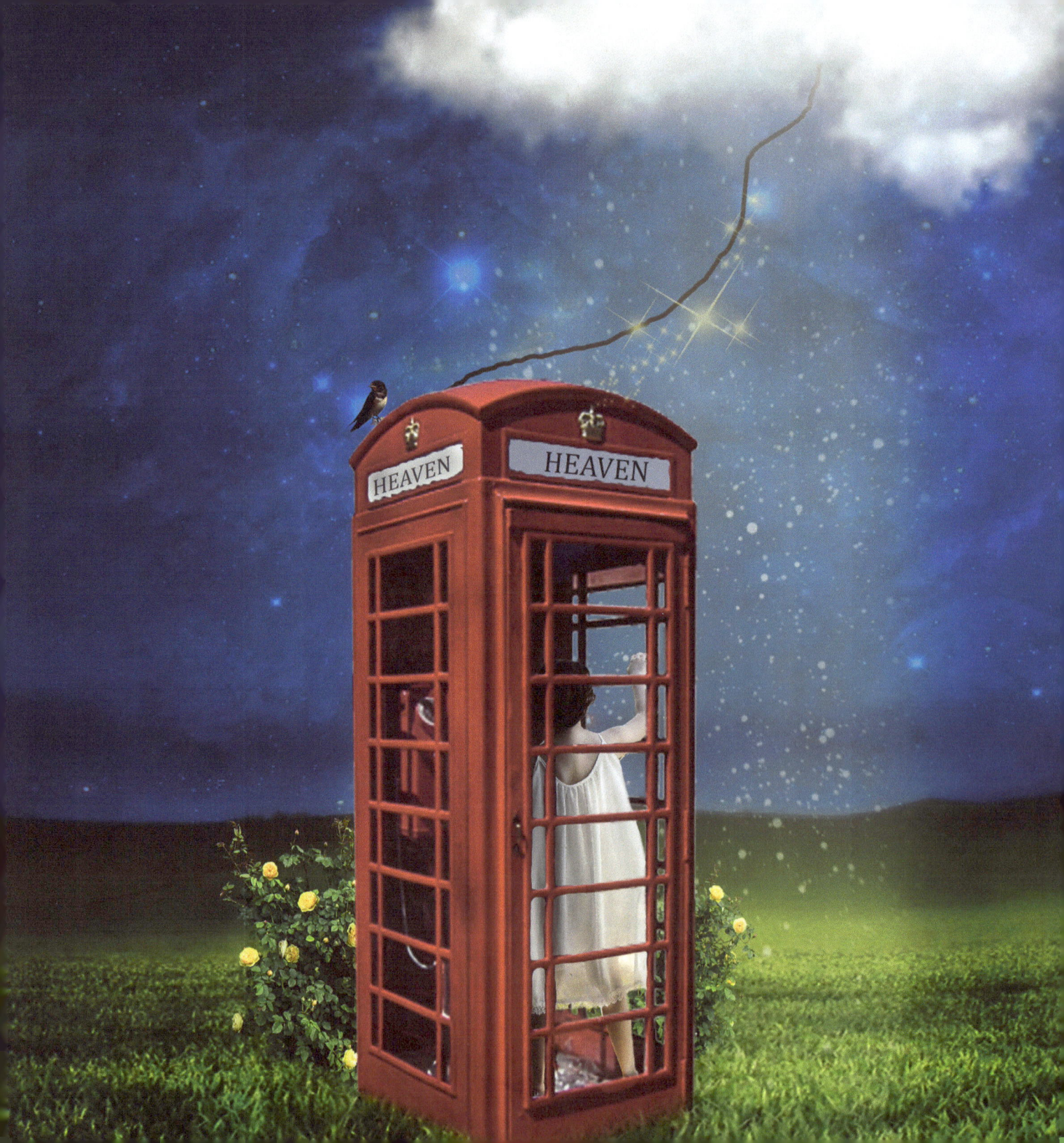

"A Phone Booth to Heaven"

My Grieving Girl,

One of the hardest things you will ever endure in life is saying goodbye. People can be here one moment, and gone the next. Our hearts are never ready for that kind of goodbye. Just know it's ok to hurt, it's ok to be angry, but you can not let it consume you. Grief is something that there are no words to express. Just a universal understanding of heartache. Don't be afraid, in those moments of grief, to reach out for comfort. Those that love you will pick you up and support you even when you feel as though everything around you is falling apart. No one likes goodbyes, but they are an undeniable part of life. Whether it be the loss of a friendship, or the loss of a loved one, heart ache will happen. It's inevitable. Do not let it put out your fire. Allow it to fuel you to move forward, to love more fiercely and to never forget the good times. And most importantly, do not allow the fear of it happening hold you back from loving with every ounce of yourself. We are creatures made from love, to love.

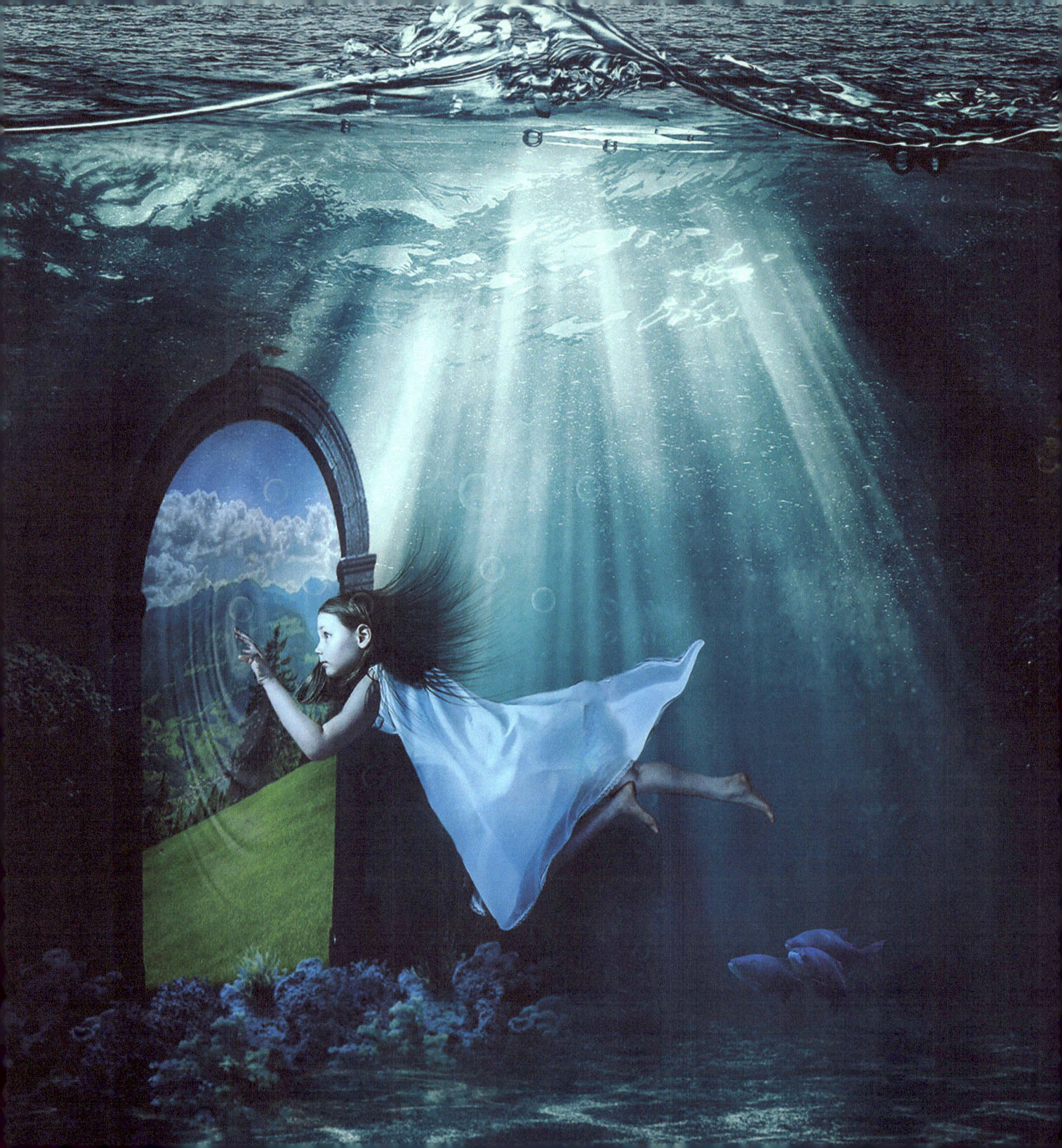

"The Gateway"

My Curious Girl

Life can bring so many different things to your table. Your curious nature and urge to learn and grow is a blessing. It means that many opportunities will be available to you, should you choose to accept them. What happens and where life takes you is all up to you. Sometimes you will be suspended in one place, looking at the reflection to what it is you truly desire, do not be afraid to push forward and discover new things. You are so incredibly brave and courageous and that will take you far in life. Don't lose track of what is most important though. Your ability to find happiness is what living life is all about. If you ever feel stuck, and happiness is faltering, keep pushing forward. It means you are not where you are meant to be at this time in your life. Just as the world around us does, our world is ever changing and growing. If you ever find that you have outgrown the place that you are at, move forward. Take that reflection that you long to be your reality and make it happen. Only you can decide what your life will be. Do not settle for less than the best and what you deserve.

"Falling"

My Perplexed Girl,

There are times in life where we don't know if we are falling up or falling down. Our worlds will flip upside down in the blink of an eye. This is part of life, this is part of growing, and how we react to these moments is going to help mold us into who we are for our whole lives. My advice to you is to always think things through. Do not act out of impulse or anger. Think things through and then react. Sometimes things may not be as they first appear, and we must take in the whole scene before we can draw a fair conclusion. Trust yourself and take the time to look at the whole picture. Be patient, and calm and you will see that there is so much more to a story than meets the eye.

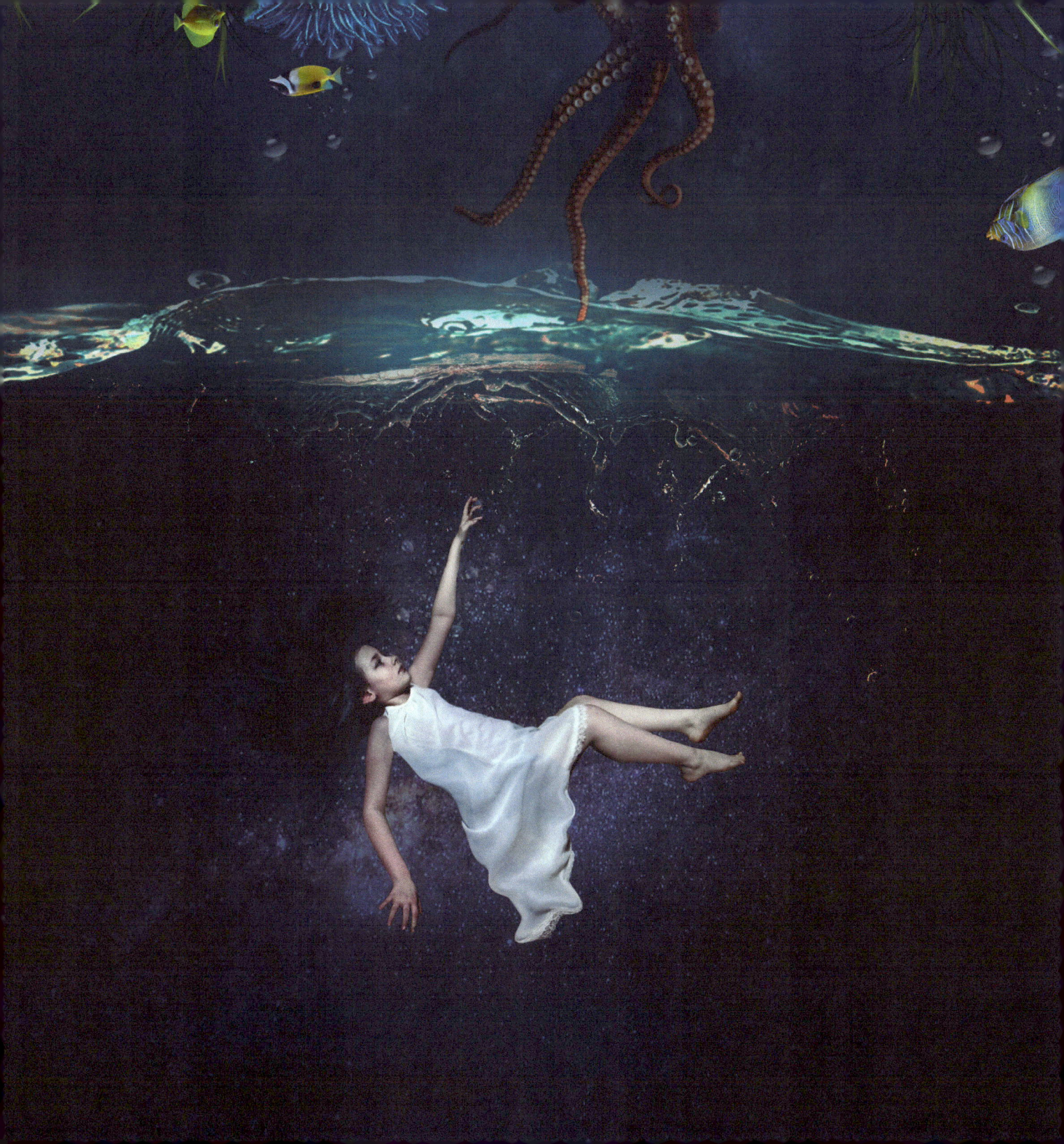

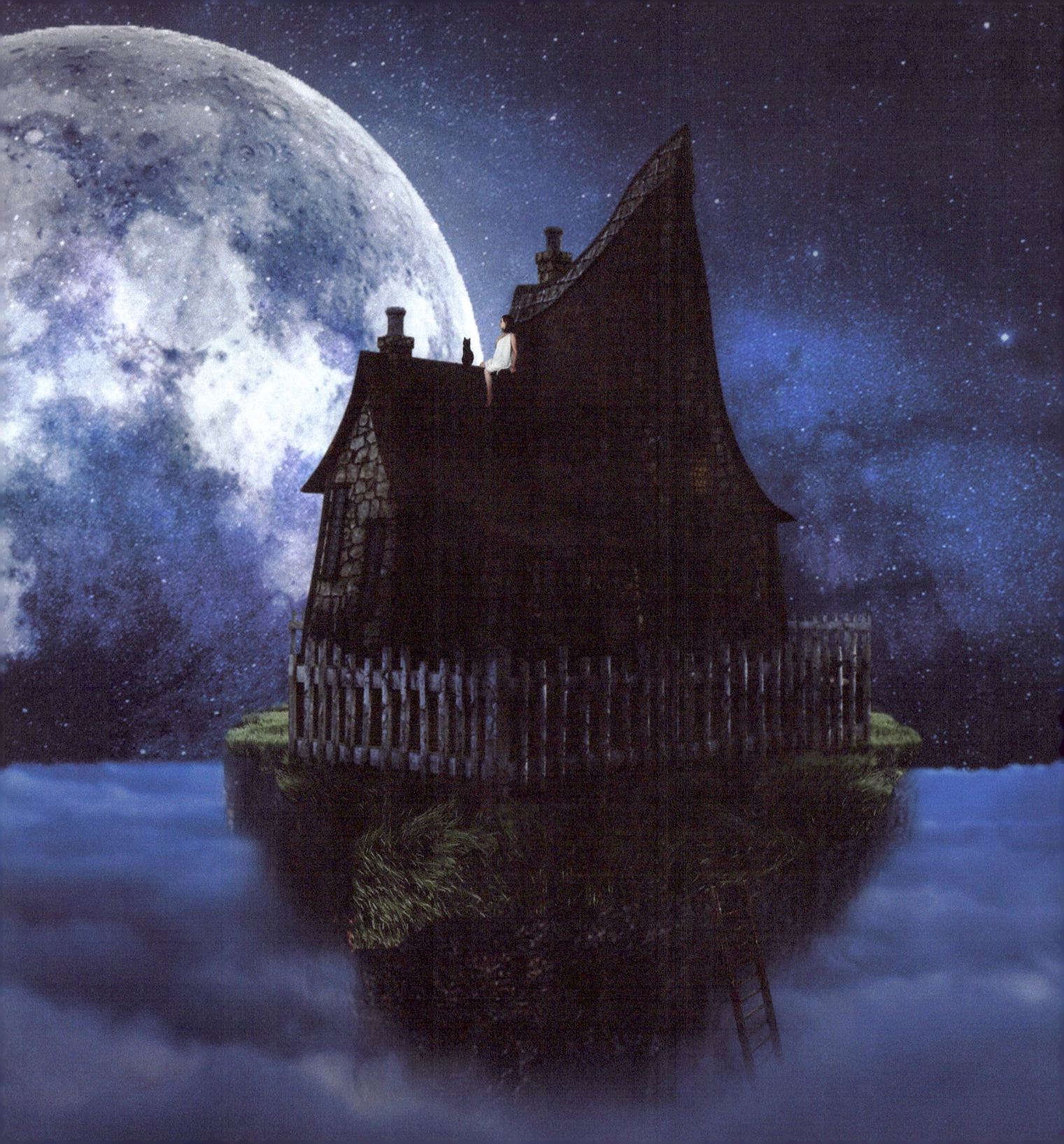

"Isolation"

My Independent Girl,

There are times where we are going to feel alone in this world. So many different things can bring about this feeling. Feeling is the key word. There is a difference between being alone and feeling alone. Being alone is something that can be a blessing. A moment of silence, a time to reflect. Feeling alone is an ache in the heart that fills you full of doubt. Remember in those moments, that you are never truly alone. Know that you are the world to me, and I will always be there for you and to love you as fiercely as you love the world around you. And don't forget, it is ok to want to spend time on your own. That is how we learn about who we are on a deeply profound level.

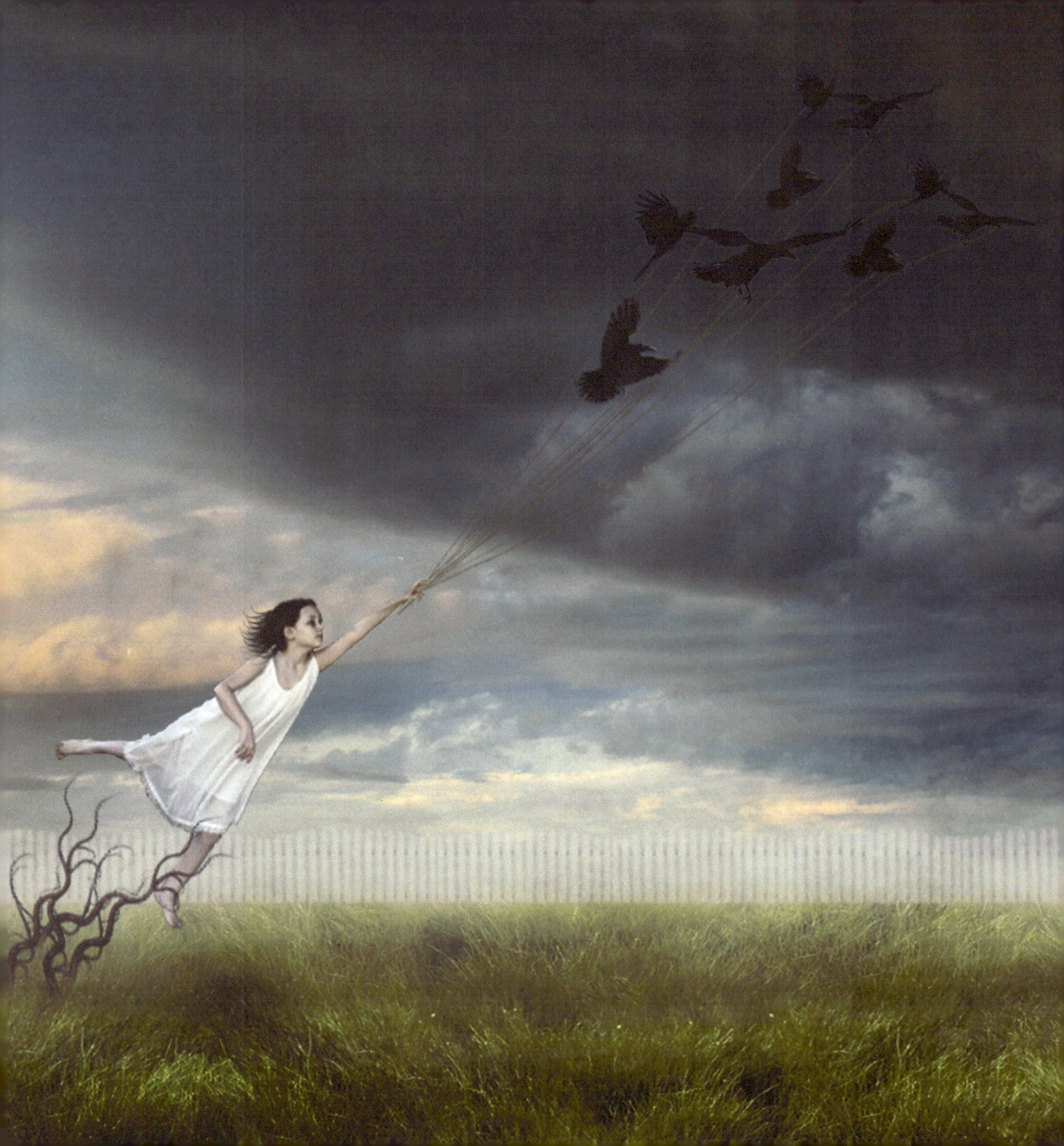

"The Escape"

My Determined Girl,

There will be so much opportunity available to you in this world. Always follow your heart and your dreams. There is only one life for us to live, and it is up to us to make the most of it. Many times we allow ourselves to become rooted down to where we are. It's ok to build roots, but just know that things and people change. If there comes a time that your roots are no longer nurturing you and helping you grow, it's time to break free and move forward. Our lives are so full of adventure, and stories yet to be told. Don't root yourself down until you are ready, and you know in your heart it is where you are meant to be. Do not allow yourself to root down in bad soil, in a place that doesn't allow you the room to grow. Always be true to yourself and you'll know when it's time to root, and when it's time to pull free and move on to greater things.

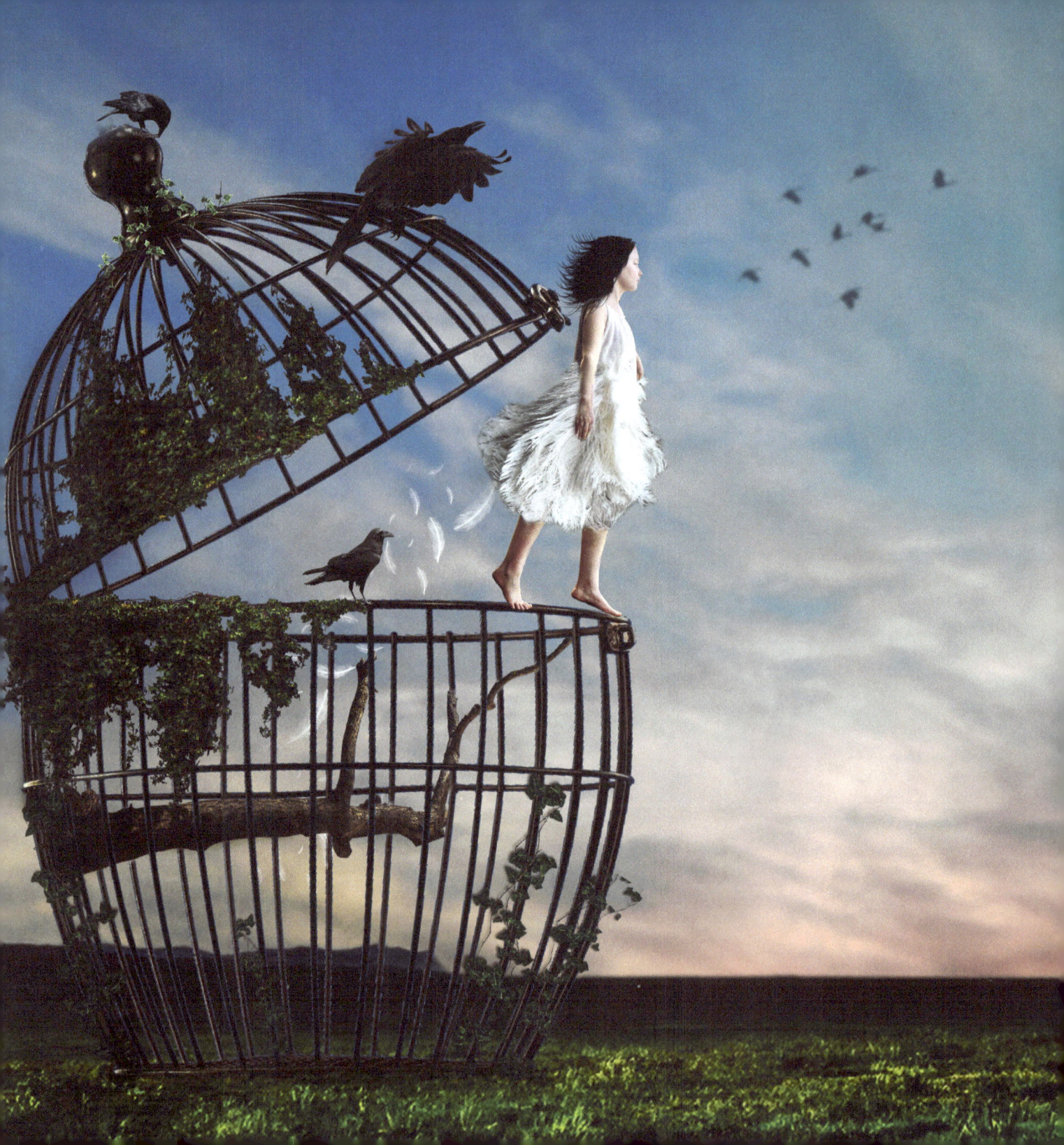

"Escape Your Cage"

My Free Spirited Girl,

It is very easy to allow ourselves to feel trapped in a cage we can not escape. We begin to welcome the security that comes with our cage, and begin to feel as though it is keeping us safe from what lurks outside the bars. Don't allow yourself to be fooled. It is still a cage. Your spirit yearns to be free, to live life to its fullest and to experience all the amazing things in this world. Do not let the false comforts of these cages bind you and tame you. Break free of the bars, and allow yourself to be who you are meant to be. Do not let anyone cage your spirit. That spirit is special to you, and is driven with purpose. Do not let the false securities of those bars bind you to a life you are just settling for. Rattle the cage. Shake the bars, and fight your way free and you will see that amazing things will happen.

"She is a Storm"

My Ferocious Girl,

Fear no storm that blows your way. Stand your ground and I promise you that you will make it through to the other side. Life will bring a variety of stormy trials that will give us moments that define who we are. Weather that storm, and don't lose sight of yourself. Learn from it, but remember to always let it blow by. What happens in that storm will shape who you will grow to be. You will face many different storms, many different moments that will define you and your life. Trust yourself, stay true to yourself, and don't fear the storm, be the storm. Be a force to be reckoned with and always hold your ground.

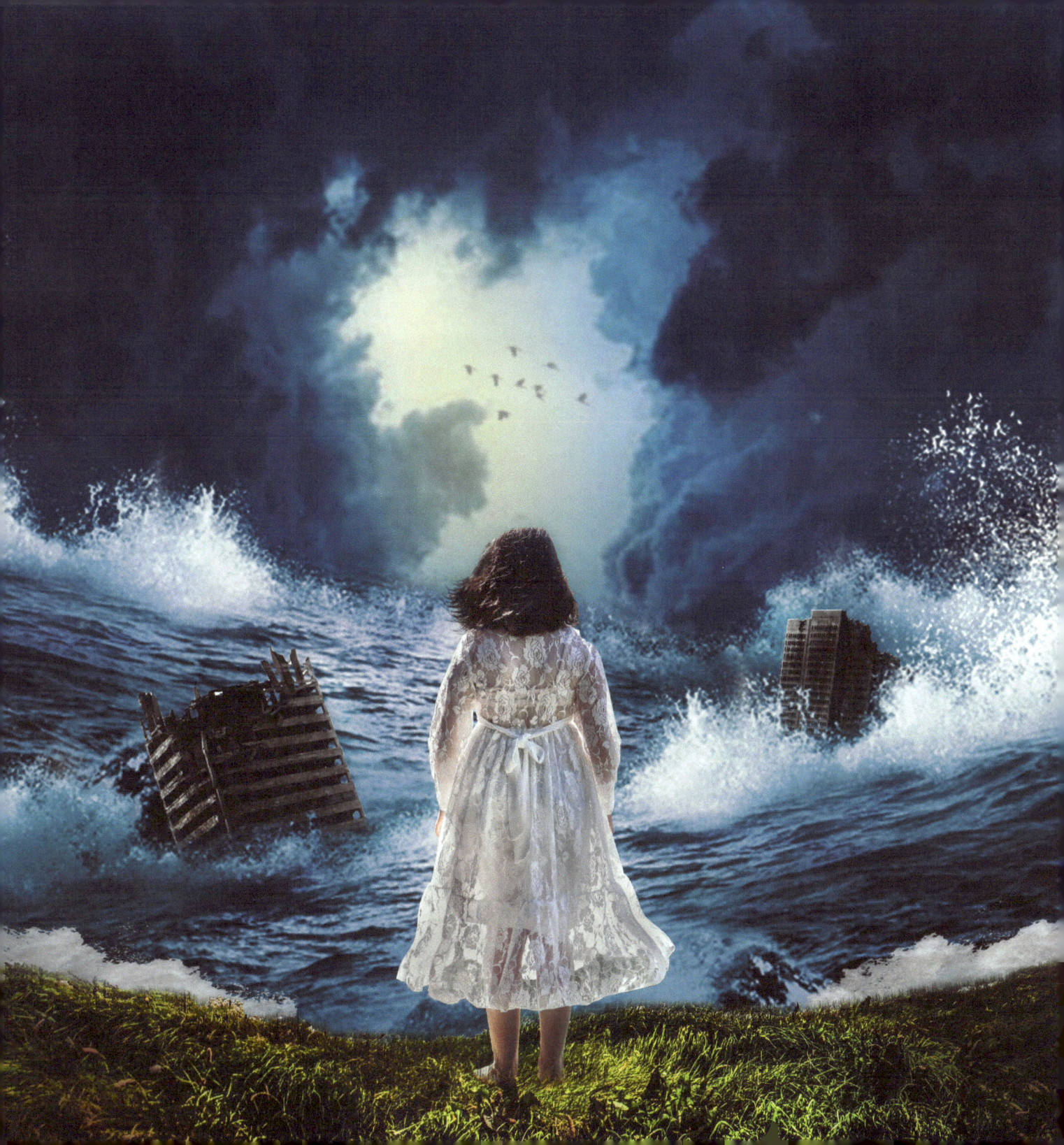

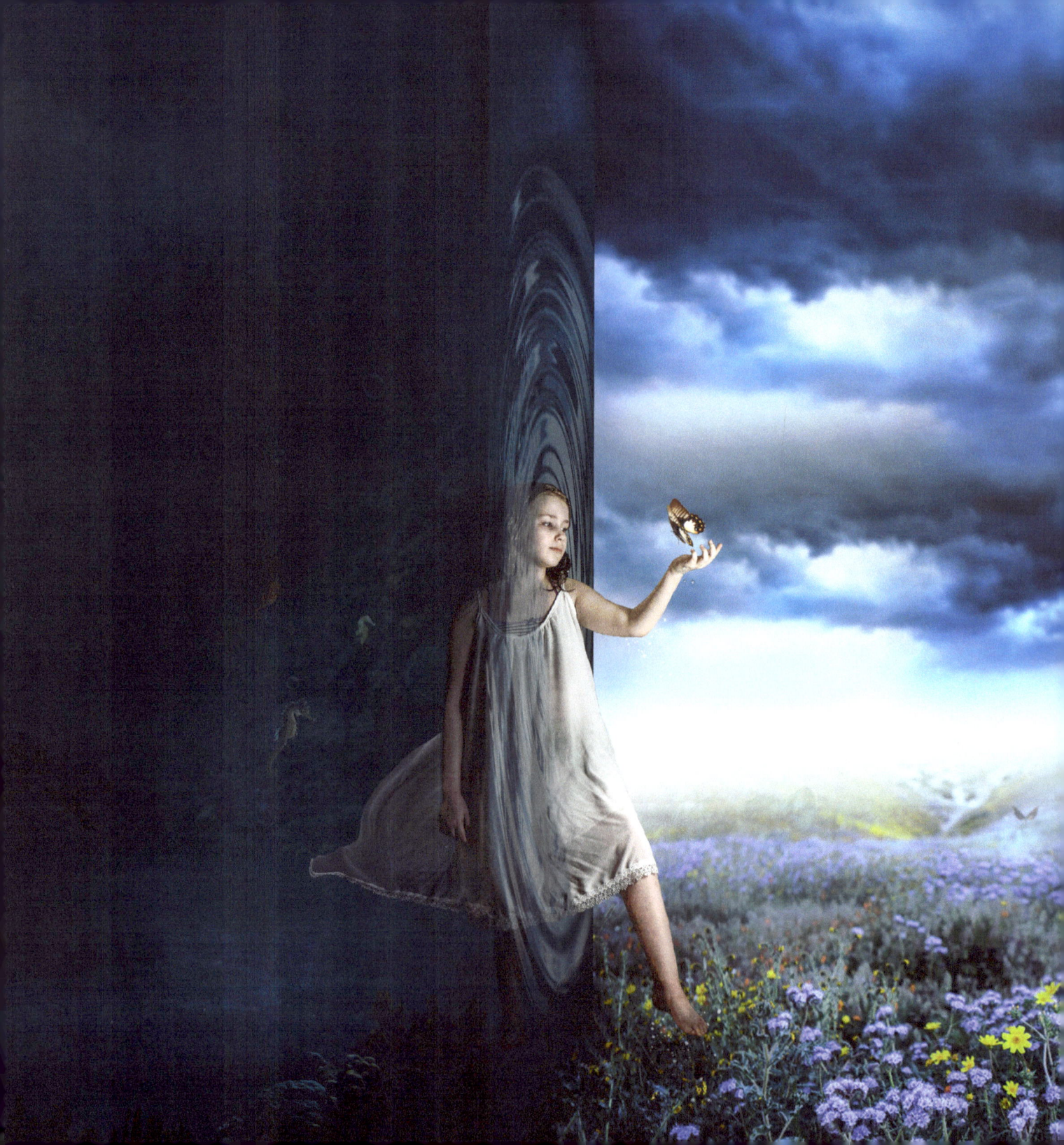

"Between Two Worlds"

My Loving Girl,

The journey of life is a never ending challenge. You will feel as though there are times where you are caught between two worlds. Follow your heart, and trust in yourself and you will always be moving forward. Continue to see the beauty that exists around you, and don't be afraid to choose a side. Just be sure it is the side you want to be on and not the one you feel obligated to be in. We constantly set limitations on ourselves, letting the fear of the unknown stop us from pressing forward. You are never stuck somewhere unless you allow yourself to be. Remember that. There is always a choice to face in life. Sometimes we may make the wrong choices in the moment, but everything is always part of a bigger story, a grander plan. Trust yourself and just know that you may not be where you want to be in that moment, but if you don't give up you will reach where you desire to be. Each of us face a different path. It is a life full of decisions. Don't tear yourself down if you choose the wrong side first, learn from it, grow and allow it to help you become the person you are meant to be.

"The Empress"

My Powerful Girl.

You are a force to be reckoned with in this world. The capabilities that you possess are endless. The only person with the ability to hold you back from anything is yourself. Recognize how amazing you are, how much power you hold, and how unstoppably driven you truly are. Do not let the rules and expectations of others drain your power. You are better than that, and you are one of the most powerful women in the world because you are smart, you are capable, and most importantly you are loved. You can make a difference. Your life is a gift. Take that gift and allow yourself to be who you are. If people don't like it, let them go. Do not give others your power as they will drain it from you ounce by ounce until there is nothing left. Own your power, own your voice and most importantly, own your life. No one can stop you once you set your mind to something. Remember that. You are able to move mountains.

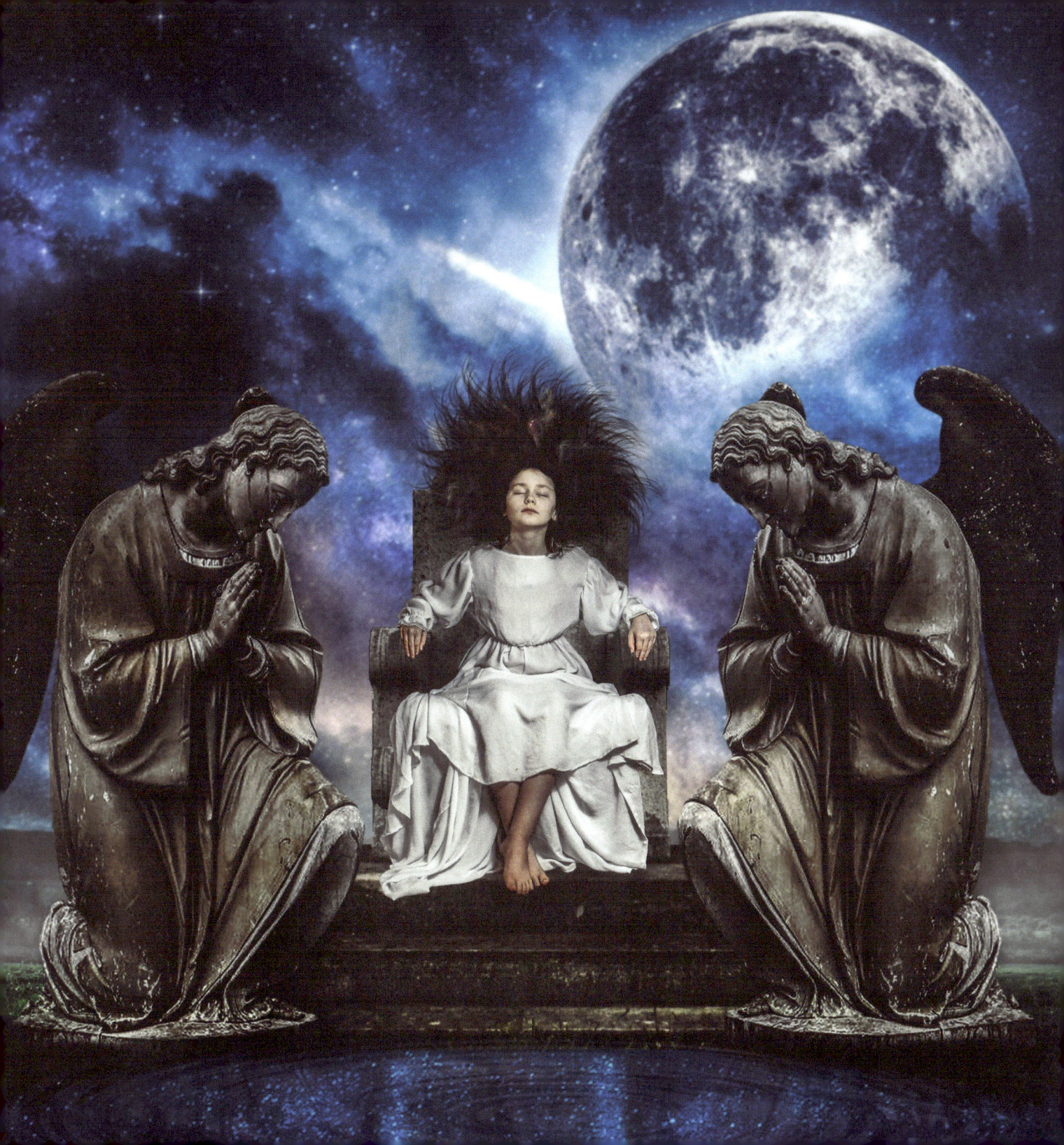

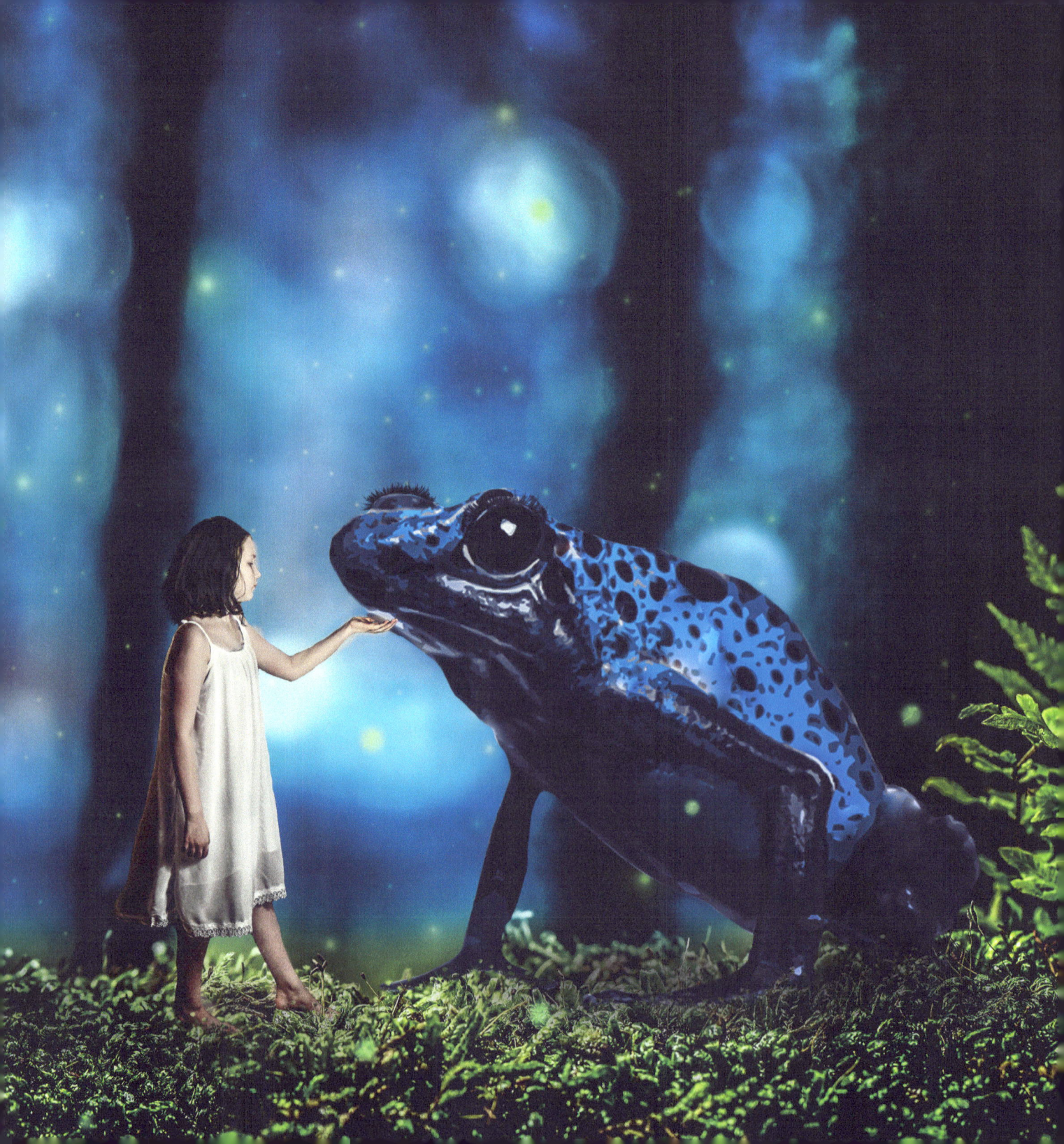

"Blue"

My Loving Girl,

Your loving nature is something that is inspiring. You love so purely and unconditionally, without questions and without fault. From the smallest snail, to the moon in the sky, your love can change the world. There will be times in your life that will make you feel that the love you generate is a burden, that it leads to heartache, and you must realize, that is all a part of life. Don't let those heartaches take away the beauty of your love. All I can ask of you is, of all the things you will love in this life, please remember to love yourself the most. As long as you continue to love yourself, it is easy to give it freely to those that deserve it. The older we get, the easier it becomes to lock that love away and keep it guarded and protected. But that is not experiencing love, that is hiding from it. Do not hide from it, because love is the most beautiful thing this life has to offer. Continue to love with all of your heart, even when it hurts sometimes, because when it all comes down to it, Love is the most important experience we can have in this world. It is responsible for molding us into who we are.

"The Next Chapter"

My Driven Girl,

Just like in any good book, look forward to the next Chapter. Some people fear new things, some people fear change. My words to you are to embrace it. With change comes growth. Don't be afraid to end a story in your life that you are done reading from. It is ok to be ready to move on to something new. Do not allow yourself to be stuck reading the same pages over and over again. That's how we become bored and restless. Turn the page, and follow the journey of this life into the next chapter. Be Brave, be strong, and trust yourself and your story. If we never move on to the next page, we can miss out on so many amazing things. Always move forward. Always look forward to what the future holds, and never stop dreaming. We only get one life to live, one story to write. Make sure you always stay true to you and your story, and never fear the future. Embrace it, boldly cross into the next chapter and you will always be right where you are supposed to be. Trust yourself and trust your story. It will have lots of twists and turns, full of ups and downs, but it is YOUR story and no one else's. You are capable of doing the most amazing things in this life. Do not let fear of the unknown stop you from moving forward. Remember that you are loved and your story is an important one.

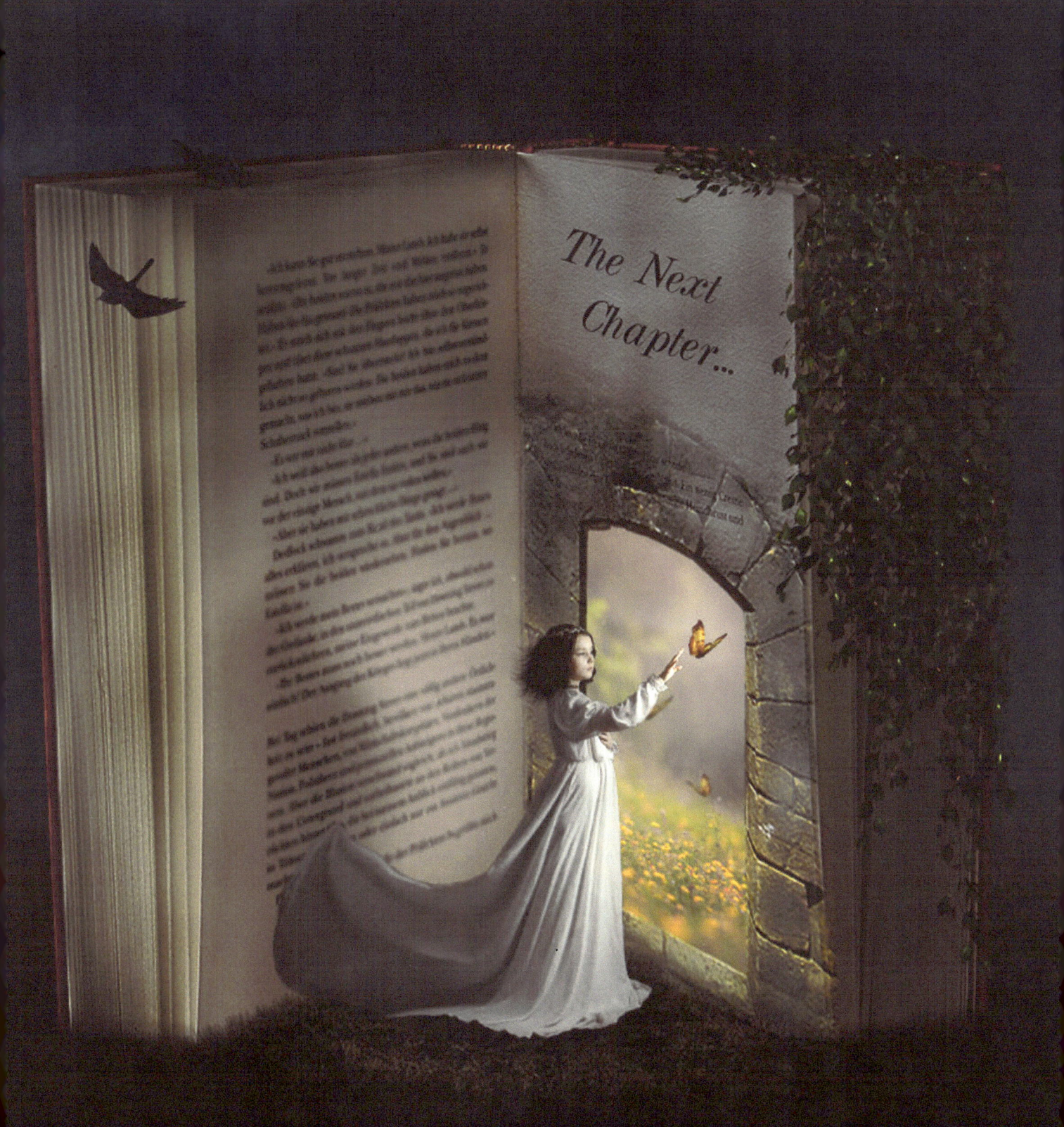

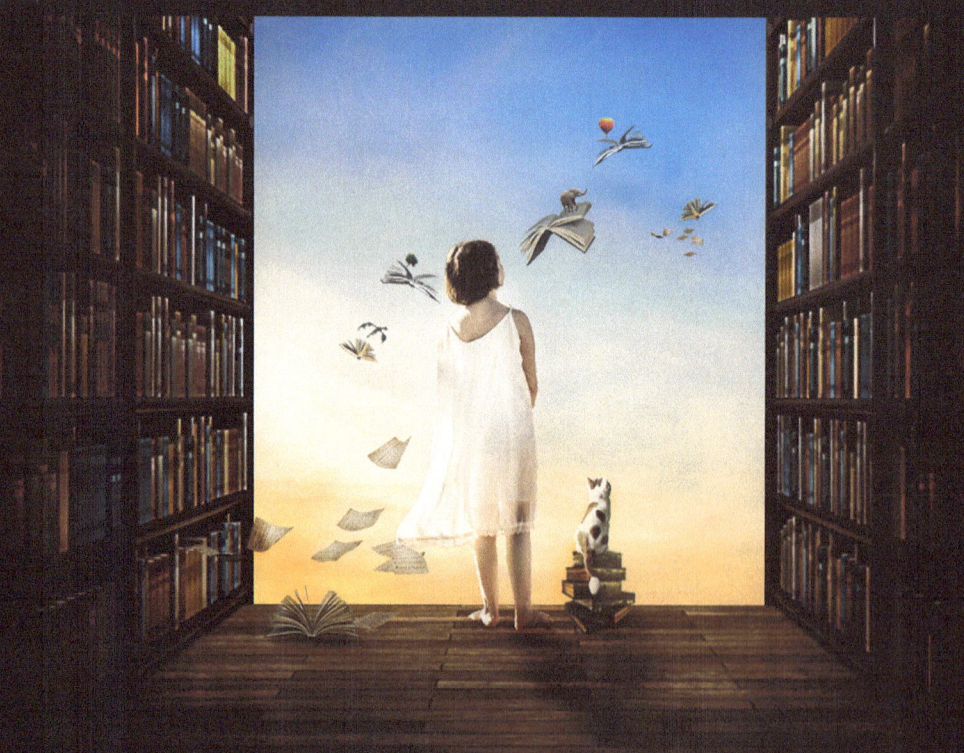

More adventures of the Girl in the White Dress to come in 2020

© Jessica Hatlen Imagery 2019

All rights reserved. No part of this publication may be reproduced, stored in a retrieval system, or transmitted in any form by any means, electronic, mechanical, photo copying, recording, otherwise without the pryer written permission of the publisher.

www.ingramcontent.com/pod-product-compliance
Lightning Source LLC
Chambersburg PA
CBHW040451220526
45473CB00004B/1596